Little Reminders

Guided grief journal & colouring book

Kate Worrall

Illustrated by Clara Spinassi

This journal belongs to

_____
NAME

and has been created in loving memory of

_____
NAME

When I think of you I feel...

I love you because...

What I miss most is...

My favourite memory of you is...

Little Reminders of things you loved...

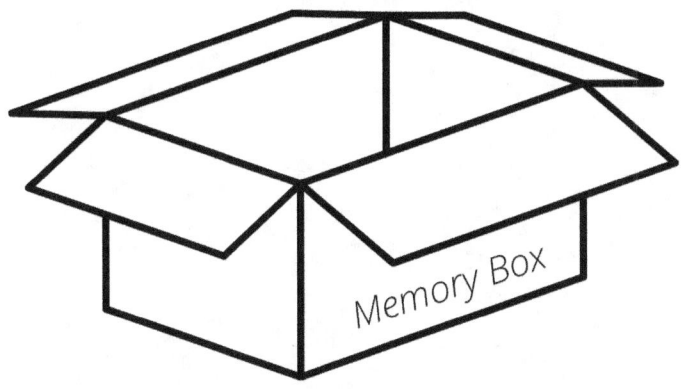

My favourite thing we used to do together was...

Your strengths were...

Find out more about strengths at www.viacharacter.org/character-strengths

My strengths are...

Identify your strengths using the free online strengths assessment at www.viacharacter.org/survey

The characteristics of you that I see in myself are…

You taught me...

I believe...

I wish...

I'm sorry for...

If I could ask you one thing it would be...

I love you and something I want you to know is…

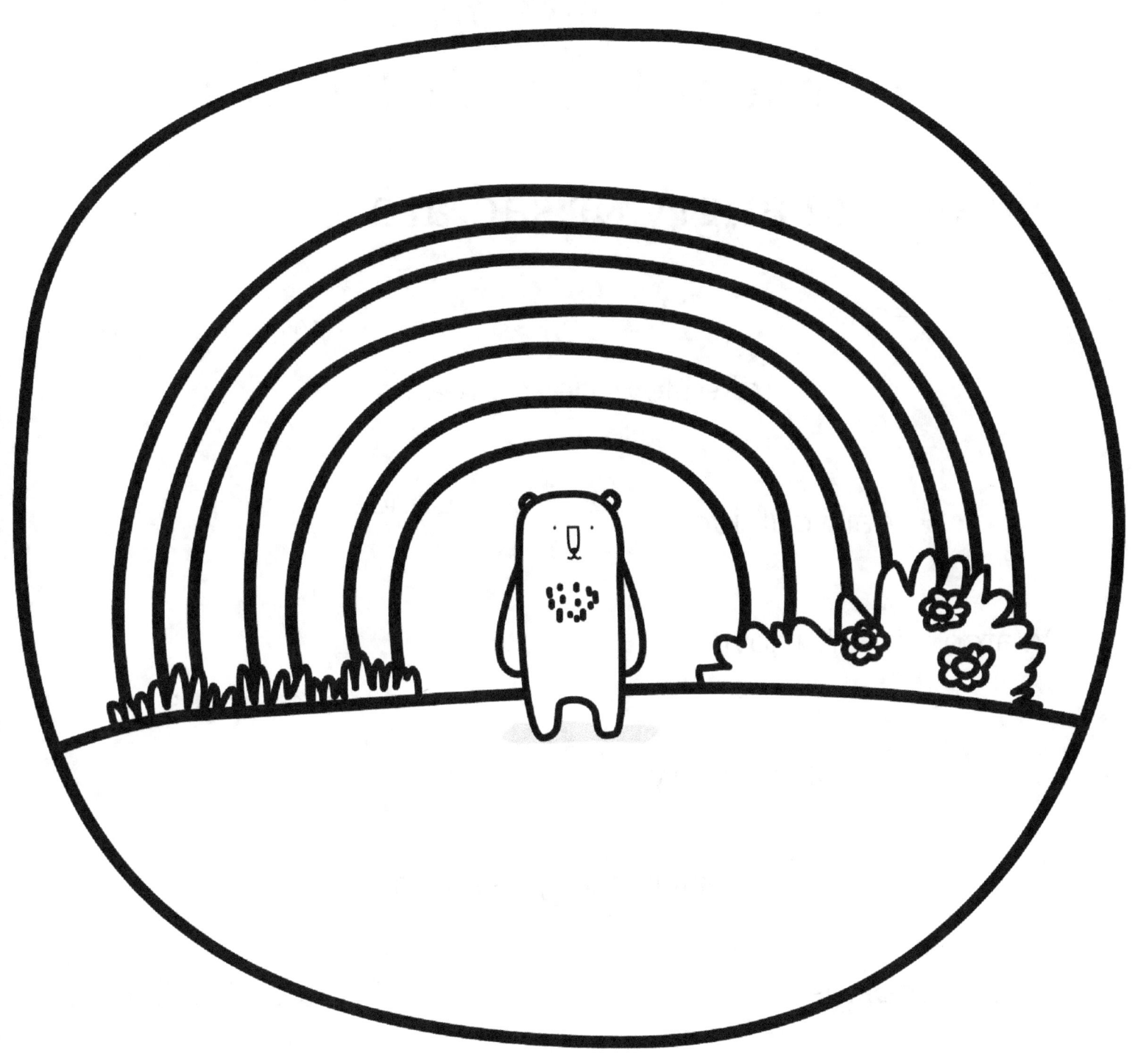

Things that make me feel better when I'm angry or sad are... (circle)

Tell someone

Write in a journal

Take slow, deep breaths

Scream outside

Dance to music

Watch a funny movie

Write a letter

Have a good cry

Walk in the grass with bare feet

Bake cookies

Walk on the beach

Play sport

Draw a picture

Play an instrument

Walk the dog

Throw rocks in the water

Run around the yard

Pat my pet

Call a friend

Spend time with family

Exercise

Tell a joke

Play at the park

Listen to music

Write a list

Write a poem

Give someone a hug

Read a good book

I think you would want me to focus

my energy on...

The things that makes me feel the safest are...

The people I can share memories and stories of you with are...

Friends :

Teachers :

Family :

Counsellors :

Neighbours :

Other :

Support groups :

Coaches :

Pets :

Ways I will remember you...

I feel close to you when...

I feel happiest when...

I am grateful for...

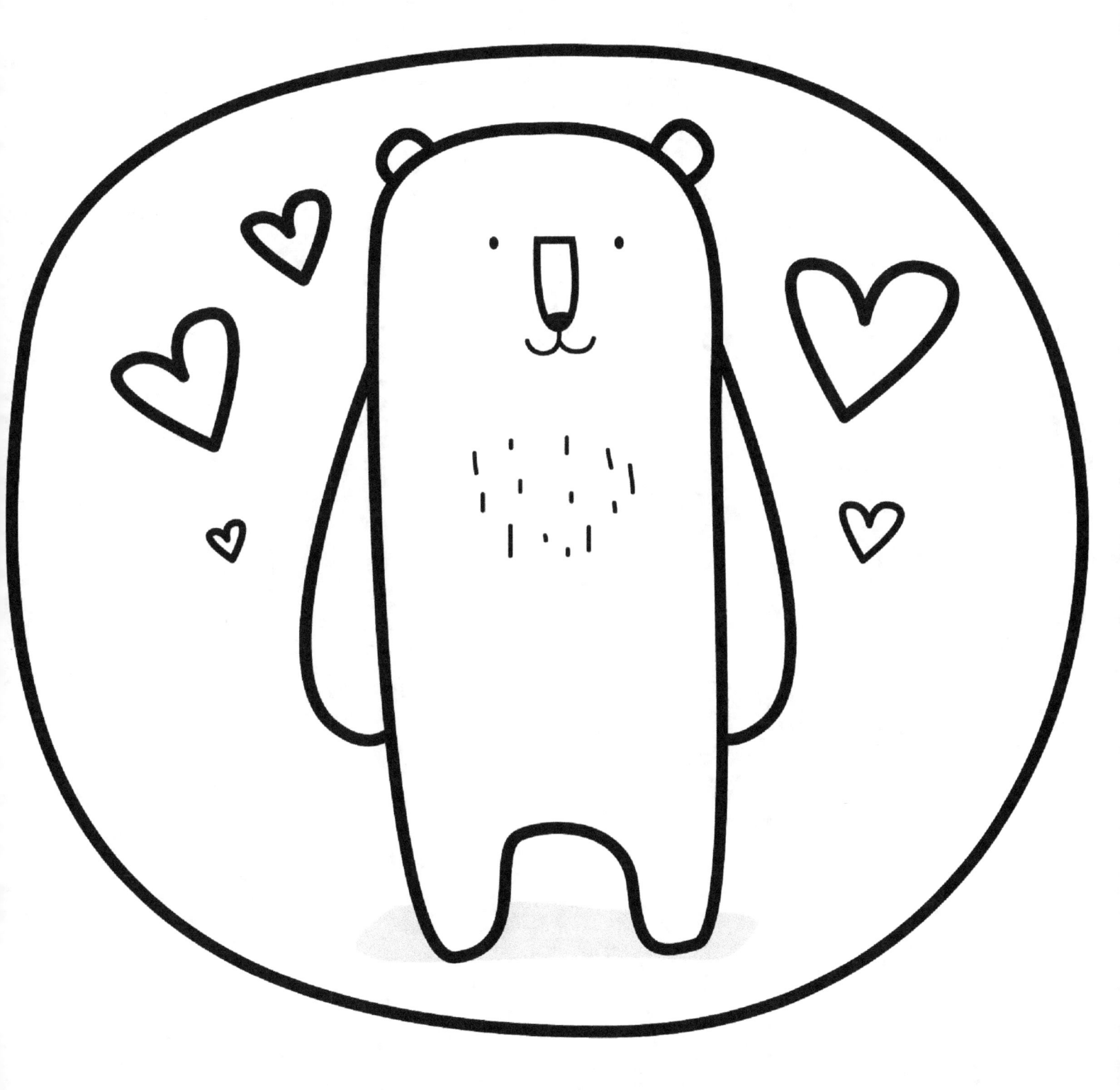

Little Reminders by Kate Worrall
Illustrated by Clara Spinassi

ISBN 978-0-6488741-1-9

Copyright © 2020 by Kate Worrall.

All rights reserved.

Newcastle, NSW Australia

Email: MyPhotoStorybooks@outlook.com
Website: www.KateWorrall.com

Without limiting the rights under copyright reserved above, no part of this publication may be reproduced, stored in or introduced into a database and retrieval system or transmitted in any form or by any means (electronic, mechanical, photocopying, recording or otherwise) without the prior written permission of both the owner of copyright and the above publishers.

www.ingramcontent.com/pod-product-compliance
Lightning Source LLC
Chambersburg PA
CBHW080847020526
44107CB00079B/2639